Camille SAINT-SAËNS

Concerto No. 1 for Cello and Orchestra in A minor, Op. 33

T0087589

PLAYBACK+
Speed • Pitch • Balance • Loop

To access audio visit:
www.halleonard.com/mylibrary

Enter Code
5506-5403-1093-7324

ISBN 978-1-59615-842-9

Exclusively Distributed By

Visit Hal Leonard Online at
www.halleonard.com

Contact us:
Hal Leonard
7777 West Bluemound Road
Milwaukee, WI 53213
Email: info@halleonard.com

In Europe, contact:
Hal Leonard Europe Limited
42 Wigmore Street
Marylebone, London, W1U 2RN
Email: info@halleonardeurope.com

In Australia, contact:
Hal Leonard Australia Pty. Ltd.
4 Lentara Court
Cheltenham, Victoria, 3192 Australia
Email: info@halleonard.com.au

SAINT-SAËNS
CELLO CONCERTO NO. 1 IN A MINOR

Camille Saint-Saëns (1835-1921)

Camille Saint-Saëns (1835-1921) first explored the cello as a solo instrument in 1862 when he composed his Suite, op. 16, but then largely neglected the instrument for the rest of the decade. In the 1870's however, his interest was renewed and in 1872 he composed his Cello Concerto no. 1 in A minor, op. 33 along with his first Cello Sonata in C minor, op. 32. These works were shortly followed by his popular Allegro Appassionato in B minor, op. 43 (1875) as well as the lesser known Romance in D major, op. 51 (1877). He would not write his second concerto (in D minor, op. 119) until 1902, thirty years after his first.

While there is no documented story that exists regarding the origin of his first cello concerto, it is known that Saint-Saëns had become acquainted with August Tolbecque, a masterful cellist who was a professor at the Conservatoire in Marseilles. Tolbecque played the solo part at the premiere in Paris on Jan. 19, 1873, and the concerto was dedicated to him.

The Cello Concerto no. 1 in A minor has an original structure as well as an attractive and challenging solo part. Although it is through-composed, it is easily divided into three movements. The main theme from the opening reappears several times in each of the sections, which gives the piece a unity and sense of organic wholeness.

1872, the year his First Cello Concerto was written, had not been a very successful year for Camille Saint-Saëns and was a period when many of his works were receiving vehement criticism. However, when it was premiered in Germany at a concert in Dresden on Nov. 24th, 1875, it was favorably received and quickly became one of his most popular works and a standard part of the classical repertory. Now, more than 140 years later, it is still considered to be one of the most important works for solo cellists.

Camille Saint-Saëns

Concerto No. 1 for Cello and Orchestra in A minor, Op. 33

Contents

Note: there is no time delay between the three movements.

Camille Saint-Saëns

Concerto No. 1 for Violoncello & Orchestra
in A minor, Opus 33

Cello

Edited by Nancy Green

MMO 3779

6

Cello

8

Cello

Cello

Cello

Cello

Cello

Cello

Cello

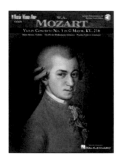

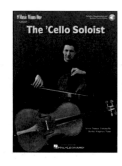
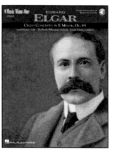
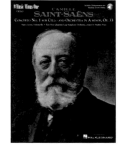

1020
199